BRIGHT FELON

WESLEYAN POETRY

Kazim Ali

BRIGHT FELON

AUTOBIOGRAPHY AND CITIES

WESLEYAN UNIVERSITY PRESS

Middletown, Connecticut

Published by

Wesleyan University Press,

Middletown, CT 06459

www.wesleyan.edu/wespress

2009 © Kazim Ali

Printed in U.S.A.

5 4 3 2 1

Portions of this work have previously
appeared in *Narwhal, Xcp: Cross-cultural
Poetics*, and *Quarter After Eight*.

Library of Congress
Cataloging-in-Publication Data
Ali, Kazim, 1971–
Bright felon: autobiography and cities /
Kazim Ali.
    p. cm.—(Wesleyan poetry)
ISBN 978-0-8195-6916-5 (cloth: alk. paper)
I. Title.
PS3601.L375B75   2009
811'.6—dc22   2009013375

Wesleyan University Press is a member of
the Green Press Initiative. The paper used in
this book meets their minimum requirement
for recycled paper.

This project is supported in part by an award
from the National Endowment for the Arts.

NATIONAL
ENDOWMENT
FOR THE ARTS
A great nation
deserves great art.

A fragment
of a fair copy would undo our slant meeting,

[. . .]

I approached
as an alias, trachea

   without sound, my signature, bright felon.

| GILLIAN CONOLEY

CONTENTS

ACKNOWLEDGMENTS

Gratitude to Meena Alexander,
brave speaker.

To the kind editorial eye, keen ear for
the phrase, and quick-slashing pen of
Joshua Marie Wilkinson.

To Marco Wilkinson, who saw me
through it.

To my cousins Haider Saeed and Laura
van Alphen, whose friendship I have
always counted on.

I am grateful also to Marilyn Nelson
and the Soul Mountain Retreat (www.
soulmountainretreat.com) for the week
in which the manuscript was finalized,
and to Suzanna Tamminen for her kind
and passionate interest.

And of course, to Jason.

November 2006 – April 2007
February 2008 – October 2008

BRIGHT FELON

MARBLE HILL

Paradise lies beneath the feet of your mother. A verse I've heard recited so frequently I do not know if it is scripture or *hadith.*

Hadith, meaning traditions of the prophet, are always accompanied by a careful oral lineage of who said what to whom, and who heard who say they heard what. Usually back to one of the prophet's wives who heard the prophet say it.

The veil also between what you want to see and cannot see, what you wish to have heard but did not hear.

In *butoh* the dancers are rendered in white smoke, ghosts traversing the stage-as-womb, moving so slowly you do not even know they are there.

If paradise lies beneath the feet of my mother then how will I find my way inside unless she admits me.

Now I look at each face, each body, as it moves around the subway platform, down the stairs and around the platform, onto trains, off of them.

After my aunt Chand-mumani's death I thought of them each as flames, in each the body is combusting, burning up the fuel of the soul.

Michelle after giving birth walked around the city imagining everyone glistening, bordered in amniotic grit.

But is it really like Fanny writes, the body only a car the soul is driving.

Or something of us sunk into the matter of the body, part of us actually flesh, inseparable from it and upon death, truly dispersed, smoke.

The body of the prophet's wife always between us. Who said what.

In which case there really is something to grieve at death: that the soul is wind, not immortal.

A middle-aged woman, in the seat in front of me on the train, wearing a green puffy winter jacket. Her hair, though pulled back, frizzy and unkempt.

It's the unkempt I feel tenderness towards.

Have always felt about myself a messiness, an awkwardness, an ugliness.

As a child, such an envy of birds, of graceful slopes, of muscular boys.

In the train rushing above ground at 125th Street. Thinking about stumbling.

House by house, walking down this street or the other one. Going into the library, going into the school.

Where every middle-aged woman is my mother.

Waiting to be trusted with the truth.

I have nearly as much silver in my hair as she does.

Any pronoun here can be misread. He can mean you can mean I.

An odd list of things I want to do in the next five years: study *butoh*. Write an autobiography. Go back to Paris. Get lost somewhere I haven't been.

Also begin to say it.

Marco and I moved to Marble Hill in the summer of 2006.

Let me tell you a story about a city that floats onto the ocean. Opposite of Atlantis which fell into the sea or Cascadia which threatens to rise back out of it.

Marble Hill, a real hill, perched at the northernmost tip of Manhattan Island, a promontory out into the conjunction of the Hudson River and Spuyten Duyvil Creek.

The wind is an instrument, its own section of the sky orchestra.

Today I read of a Turkish mullah who is canceling 800 different *hadith* regarding treatment of women found now or believed at least to be untrue.

Untrue is it.

Untrue the laws that were graven in fire or graven in stone.

Says the Quran, "This is the Book. In it there is no doubt."

All for a belief that a human animal is a wicked one and requires a law.

Which requires if not actual violence then at least the threat of it.

At least fury.

Here in Marble Hill you are where you aren't.

Orchestral the river that curves and curves north of the island.

Ships bound for the upper east side from Albany have a harder and harder time negotiating the torturous and twisting Spuyten Duyvil.

So a canal is blasted through and what was once the northern tip of Manhattan became an island.

Walking across one of the bridges in Paris I came to a place called Les Mauvais Garçons. Being afraid to enter I crossed the street to another tavern.

I stayed for three hours.

Radiant with traffic, the streets do not remember the gone.

The pillar at the Place de Bastille does not put back brick or bar.

Ten miles out of Chartres nothing but grain across and gray above a dark raven emerges screaming from the fields.

These thoughts are nothing, following one after the other.

Somali lesbians scheduled for their execution. Two boys in Iran convicted of drunken and lewd behavior and hanged for it. Boys. 16 and 18. There was video footage of the actual hanging on the internet.

I watched it myself.

"You wear your fingers down copying sacred texts," sang Lalla, "but still the rage inside you has no way to leave."

The Arabic line "This is the Book. In it there is no doubt" can also be read as "This is, no doubt, the Book . . . "

Dear mother, there is a folder of my loose poems lost somewhere during the summer of 2006 when I traveled between Pennsylvania, New York City, Virginia, Maine, and your house in Buffalo. There was a letter inside the folder to you.

Though I've looked and looked and failed to find it, I am sure it is still in the house in Buffalo somewhere. An envelope with a folder inside. Inside the folder loose poems. Tucked into poems, there was a letter.

The veil between what you want to see and what you cannot see.

Emily Dickinson sent her first letter to Thomas Higginson unsigned. She included with the unsigned letter a smaller sealed envelope in which there was a calling card upon which she had written her name.

When Colin Powell spoke at the UN about the invasion of Iraq, workers were asked to hang a black drape over Picasso's *Guernica*.

Which would have otherwise been in the background, surrounding him, as he spoke.

There is a body and a boy between you and utterance, the boy you were who could never speak.

Bright red bracelet of time.

"Fury," is how Galway Kinnell explained Dickinson's intent in writing her poems.

Poetry and fury in the time of war. Civil War for her.

What is my war? Not the one you think.

I won't say.

Constant state, sure as the white noise on the television after the station has gone off the air.

But who goes off the air any more.

And whose air.

Come to Marble Hill then.

Each night sleep is pierced by someone outside gunning their car engine over and over again before driving off.

A car alarm or two.

There is a streetlight outside the window that shines into the bedroom, bright as the moon but more orange.

Orange like the saffron scarf I wore to *Tokudo.* — "leaving home." When Ansho became a monk and took a new name.

The day I sat down next to a young man with a sweet smile. A gardener. Name of Marco.

The train runs the next block over. We are on the second floor so hear it if we really pay attention.

By now its rumble on the tracks, the chiming when the doors are about to close, are on the order of background noise.

I have not yet learned how to sleep through the night.

Marble Hill was an island for twenty years before the Spuyten Duyvil Creek, still running, underground below 228th Street, was filled in and joined to the mainland.

The city itself, my life, that first *butoh* performance I saw.

A man with such slow and intense movements, so internal.

You hardly knew he had moved at all and suddenly he was all the way across the stage, contorted, holding a glass bowl aloft in which a fish swam.

None of which you had even noticed was on the stage.

As I write this, a car alarm. The train.

Then silence.

CARLISLE

Because what I think is that this tender beast, brown-skinned animal
grotesque and lustful, is me and my immortal soul besides.

In Carlisle I have two writing desks on opposite sides of the room, one
the pecan-wood desk with the nicks on the thin legs, the deer legs. The
other the butler-desk with grill-covered bookshelves built into the sides.

Both of these I bought with money from my first real job when I moved
north of the city to Rhinebeck.

A part of the story I haven't gotten to yet. Though it was already
years ago.

Always in the broken story there is more to tell.

Mornings I rise in the cold and walk two blocks down to the
old colonial graveyard to read history in the broken stones, names
sometimes worn away, the stories of first wives, second wives,
dead infants and unmarked whose.

In this way read the history of the place.

The history of any place for me is simple: a route between my home on
South Bedford Street, across the main intersection to the coffee shop on
the corner of Pitt and High Street.

The other compass points are the independent bookstore, the used
bookstore, a house on Hanover Street where Marianne Moore lived,
and a strange park that was once a graveyard.

On the north side of town, a place where the land was broken and
bones disturbed.

Details on the display plaques in that park are sketchy and will lead me into shadowed places — the town records, rooms I've never been.

But I don't discover this small park near the railroad tracks with its distressing history until I've lived in the town more than seven months.

In the body of a tree I hear a resonance. While out in space between planets lie cores of planets.

An iron fence grows through the heart of the tree; I pass it every day in the morning when I walk.

You were saying something.

You hardly pass a night that winter without sneaking out into the hallway and turning the thermostat up four or five degrees.

Eating baked beans out of a can with couscous for dinner nearly every night. Not because you live alone or don't have the time to take care of yourself better.

But because you like the taste of it.

What I learned is that each asteroid is held in careful place by a partner in space. If such a body didn't exist the orbital patterns of these same can be extrapolated graphically.

A discovery which pleases me almost as much as when I learned that every cubic equation actually has an associated modular form.

But is the reverse true.

And what has all this to do with.

Carlisle, Pennsylvania. Once a frontier town. But constructed at the frontier with specific intent.

To push the boundaries of the state out to Cumberland Pass.

I wrote an autobiography once in letters. To someone. In which I found
myself unable to actually say anything so I tried saying it in two or three
or four different versions. Eventually leaving all the various versions in.

Called it *The Historical Need for Music.* Or was that *Hysterical Need.*

Repeating the chapters in different variations so I could speak out
of both sides of my mouth, not because I wanted to evade but because
I didn't know what really happened.

The County Jail, gothic, redstone, still stands at the corner of
Bedford and High Streets, though is offices now, the insides completely
refurbished with industrial grey carpeting, drop ceilings, and fluorescent
lights.

You have to squint at it to be fearful, though death it still tells — a
white man crushed in riots when he tried to sue for the return of two
of his slaves that had escaped north.

Needing to check whether or not he won his case. The question of
"law" vs. "morality" being what interests me.

To live in a frontier town at any rate or a town that was built on what
was supposed to be the frontier.

Later all the promises were broken and the settlements spread into
the territories.

It's always the broken that holds the universe in place.

That's what I would say about poetry and prayer.

That god or audience — the intended direction of both of those —
we wish and wish are real.

In the mornings of the late fall when it is cold enough to feel the winter beginning I would leave the house very early and walk south on Bedford Street into the old cemetery.

Here's the closest place you come in America to a city piled on top of a city.

Not like that in Cairo where the city sedimented itself and we walked down the Greek streets themselves, saw the churches hidden underground, accessible only by otherwise unmarked staircases in empty courtyards.

Through the cemetery I read the fate of the village, the deaths, the family trees, the broken headstones. How we will all break.

When I speak about my body's life I know it is brothered and descended from but do not know if blood will descend from my blood.

Does a family break or can it like water evaporate and condense and so will I then be a father in a million different ways.

Leaving the cemetery I walk through the old districts to the north side of town and after crossing the railroad tracks find a park there which is really another cemetery.

Or was — the graves now all dug up, replaced by a small green park.

One grave, surrounded by a small iron fence remains. The granddaughter of this man lived across the street and when the park was planned she battled to have this grave protected and so it was.

The others, descendantless, have disappeared, the headstones, shattered and removed, the ground planted over.

As I walk I realize, likely the bodies and bones remain, deep underground, dissipating.

You know without explanation whose graveyard that was that was torn up. You understand the color of their skin that enabled their desecration and what station they occupied in this community while they lived.

Why should I spell out every little thing.

There are things about a person's body you do not know, the things it craves and loves. All the sordid things we could never tell, the cheap things, tawdry and paltry.

Carlisle where soldiers are trained and Indians were brought to be forced to forget.

Never did I think when I arrived there that it would be the place I would sort myself out and dare actually to speak.

Nothing happened there but time.

Going in the morning to the coffee shop to read or to write.

How ordinary the most important things are.

The green copper roofs of the buildings against the steel blue-gray of the Central Pennsylvania sky. You could look at anything and understand.

In the sky, in the rain-wet street, in the palm of your hand.

Is always what you promised. What you promised is to understand.

Maybe you're never going to get there.

I thought I wouldn't get there unless I spoke, unless I told about the people I loved, the picture I drew against the corner of the room.

I'm trying to tell you how ridiculously hard it was to even try to open my mouth, to make words let alone sentences. How silence can fill every space.

To drown in a river or to lift the water up and let the drowning be your guide.

I trudge along the street unbaptized and criminal according to some religious laws.

Lonely brother, middle child, only son.

Is it written on my skin, my friend asks. Is that why you could never go on pilgrimage, never go to Mecca.

Why is it I would want go to Mecca. Because there a stone fell from the sky.

But more importantly than that small thing. That is where a mother refused to believe.

A mother refused to believe the obvious: I am alone in the desert with my son.

His breath rattles in his throat.

We have been left here by the patriarch who promised to return.

Sound familiar.

He left us and we were promised by god to safety.

This is the question of faith on the frontier.

You were promised deliverance yet there you are, no water in sight.

Do you sit and wait for the angel to either spell it all out into your ears or perhaps write it onto your skin.

Yet I think it is already written on my face, written into every corner as many times as I could say it.

There must be water around here somewhere.

Yet it isn't panic to leave a baby even then in the moment of dying.

Isn't. Is it.

And that's how it happened. God wouldn't spell it out.

Rather the water came exactly where she put the boy down.

After she risked it all for the impossible: water in the desert.

In the desert the mother was left.

She had to decide.

Do you wait for god to tell you what to do.

Or do you panic.

BEACON

You wouldn't think I would have wanted a beacon. Rather to find myself
in the wilderness on my own.

But I did, I always did.

Could there have been someone else like me, not one thing not another,
barely able to choose.

A poet, a Muslim, and of a particular persuasion.

When I knew someone like me I barely knew him and we couldn't
bring ourselves to speak of the one thing we needed to speak to each
other about.

Silence stretched between us taut as sin.

In 2004 I moved with Marco down the river to Beacon, NY.

Named for the signal fires placed on top of each mountain in a chain
running from New York City to Albany.

So if either city fell to the British the insurgents at the other end would
know about it.

I placed signal fires up and down each street, so anxious was I to belong
somewhere.

When I first arrived I quickly constructed my life, visiting the post
office, the bank, the coffee shop, the yoga studio, the used bookstore,
all nearly every day.

We lived on the third floor, our apartment overlooking one of the
municipal parking lots.

Next to a theater long since abandoned and now colonized by grackles,
thousands of them shouting.

It had to be explained to me that the sound of grackles was considered
unattractive. I found music in the noise.

Also a badger or some creature would walk over the neighboring
rooftops onto our deck to eat Marco's rare succulent plants.

A crowd of carpenter bees arrived in the spring to devour the wooden
deck.

I was not content with Marco's explanation that they were not interested
in me, so at last he hung deer net around the balcony.

The morning glory and other climbing plants soon made use of the net
and we were encased in shadowy green.

Years later I would be stung again and again by a crew of distressed
yellowjackets. Marco picked them off me one by one.

I passed *Masjid-e-Rashid,* the storefront mosque, every day on my way
to the post office.

Where an older Arab man, between the age of my mother and my
father, worked. He would occasionally ask about my background.

When I told him I was muslim, my name Kazim, he invited me to
the mosque.

When I did not appear he would ask me about it when next I went to
the post office.

Following one of the Islamic tenets: "enjoin others to good deeds."

Since I went in during working hours he knew I could have made it to the *jummah* prayers if I preferred to.

Down next to the river I went with Fanny to the Agnes Martin room.

Where suspended in time transfixed, the river turns on itself.

Flowing down to the sea, also up from the sea, an uncertain place.

I wrote it on paper five years before I drove out of the city north.

It was a light place, painted white with the graphite marks on it.

I had been there, the end of time, the place space bends around itself.

Been there looking through a painting like you look through a wall.
In this way sometimes people see heaven.

The name of the place was "through."

From the blank that only blank can give, a field without end.

Looking away and then looking back into it you could start to discern the landscape in it, the horizontal.

A little autobiography littered on the surface.

What it would have been like had I at last been able to see.

Bent into the syntax of what comes after what and what did what.

Always you are either the one looking at the painting or you are the one who made the painting.

Listen, hasn't it ever occurred to you.

The ocean gathered together at a place on the horizon you could not discern.

You always wanted to know that actual place.

You could be he or I could be.

Could be that place where the river turns and returns where I quit my metaphor and make me.

Unveiled I want to go into the water, to the place at the horizon, place the gray of the ocean and the gray of the sky could not be separated from one another.

Each are flames on a subway platform getting on and off trains and burning ourselves to the ground.

Staring into a painting you can forget.

What are we then signal fires.

Who are we and when in time, bordered in amniotic grit.

If we are in time then we are events set into motion when and by whom.

Only one room over the white blanketed fields are going to give way to black buttons slipping themselves each into a hole.

Button you up.

My body isn't itself anymore. Streams rush up one arm and down the other leg.

Can you stand with arms overhead for a year or more. You could.

December 13, 1978. March 8, 1983. Continue writing them in white on blank ink. In whatever language or whatever country.

I will bend down and press my forehead to the earth.

A brick went through the storefront window of *Masjid-e-Rashid*.

God whispers up from the earth and I want to hear it.

And believed I could hear it if I listen closely, if one foot is folded against the other — left on top, right against the earth.

Or only if I pronounced the syllables in the correct way.

Though in Urdu a consonant is one way, in Arabic another.

There is an Arabic consonant in the middle of my name I cannot pronounce. A vowel in my last name my throat cannot manage.

Someone else with my name or my face in an other country in the world, living my life. He managed it without hurting anyone, without lying.

I didn't lie he said. I managed to skirt my way around the truth.

But she asked you once didn't she. She asked you one morning after opening your bedroom door.

No. I only wished she asked me. She never asked me. Not until weeks later did she bring it up by which point I was already too afraid to say anything.

I can't even properly say my own name.

You could set yourself aflame. Your house aflame.

The wire drawn from the streetlamps in upper Manhattan, lamp to lamp to make a house.

What other house can there be, only son.

You are the only son of your father.

How will you say it seven plagues.

Plague him to tell you. The dates that are painted on black ink bracket you.

Remember why Djuna burned her books on the sinking boat: because none of them prepared her for the moment in which she was asked to burn them.

At Dia, after the Agnes Martin room, you walked past ruined continents and upended mountains, walked between gates of yarn to the dark spaces in the ground. Fanny said, this part is like Hell.

Who knows what Hell is.

A brick through the window of a house of worship. How can I care if I never went.

The conflagration in the heart of a son who disappoints his parents.

Scripture or rupture you will never know.

Paradise lies beneath this unsaid.

Blank ink and white paint, ocean and gashing sky.

On our way out of the museum, Fanny said, Well, we should to go back to the Agnes Martin room so we can end it in light.

RHINEBECK

I followed the sound of OM north from the city through tree-lined
streets.

That you could lock a secret or a memory into your stomach or chest
and still reach for the end of the universe with the other hand.

Felt haunted sliding through space north from the city upriver.

Coming from Cairo where one city was built on top of another and
another and another for a thousand years.

Still, as far as cities go, recent.

The hotel built in the Egyptian style built around a central courtyard
with a swimming pool. Whose steam room had become unbeknownst
to me a meeting place for gay Cairenes driven from the usual haunt on
one of the floating casinos by a police raid which occurred two months
before my arrival.

Resulting in the arrest of some fifty men whose trial would stretch out
for years and years.

Called the Cairo 52. Half were acquitted and the other half convicted in
March 2003.

Before or after the war?

Which half do I wish to love, the acquitted or convicted?

Half I fill my body with breath half I hold it.

Half is for the sun and half for the moon.

Haunted then all the way up the river, sheathed in ghost-energy and the red-gold leaves falling from the trees, Perseids cutting the sky across in sentences like slashing knives.

Spiral the breath and energy of the earth you reach still for what has already gone.

Years gone.

A window at the top of your head.

Sondra bent down and put her hands on my shoulder blades pushing them down from my shoulders.

What did I know about the earth until I came into this orange and red painted room.

What did I know about the body until Sondra cradled my neck in her hands and whispered to me to breathe.

When the earth was water or water was earth. In California seeing the sediment pressed sideways and vertical.

Knowing the valleys were pushed up from the ocean, first one then the other, and it was that soil that was able to produce the grapes for wine.

Every event so long after the other that history itself is hardly a chain but a conflation or a conflagration.

Where have I heard that word before.

Words whispered in the empty room but for breath.

Breath above the streets and the road I walked.

I learned to breathe here as the season turned to fall then fog and then the white fire in the night clinging to all the green edges.

Morning's white amendments, wandering on the shoulder of the road watching autumn drag itself, limping over the stile, shredding itself on the nails, fleeing west.

Coming downstairs to the health food store beneath the apartment to buy peaches, goat's milk yogurt, ginger beer, brazil nuts, seitan, tea.

Go back upstairs to work.

An empty set of sentences or syntax. Being then unable to make sentences.

Having left just prior to the skyline's collapse. I would continue to take the train back to the city to meet friends, to attend readings, to ask or to wonder.

I'm still hardly carrying it down, one thought and then another, trying to relive it.

Echinacea planted in the bed in front of the salon, across the parking lot.

Went to see the Maya Deren documentary at the independent movie house. Surprised by her voice. Wholly human, wholly ordinary, neither dark nor stark, the expected voice of a prophet.

There was an abandoned lot at the heart of town, plastic pennons strung from phone pole to phone pole so I imagined it used to be a used car lot.

I would walk a half mile up Route 9 to the fairgrounds to see the car show, or the antique show or in the summer, the county fair.

At the Laundromat I sit washing clothes, reading *A Border Comedy.*

If only.

No Horse Tack in the Machines.

That's a new thing: to actually hear what is being said around you.

In Rhinebeck I started to breathe.

Rhinebeck I came to know.

I lay down in the graveyard, hinged there.

Walking down Broadway the other day from Marble Hill to Inwood Park, not to go to the park but to get another key to my apartment which I had locked myself out of.

I saw a man, lying down on a park bench talking to himself, quite conversationally, quite matter-of-fact, "You really don't know yourself so well."

Like me mismatching his pronouns: you could mean I.

Or again downtown, a man saying to a woman as they are walking across the street in a very low and matter-of-fact tone, "I have to tell you the most amazing thing."

Because we are pressed against each other on the train it is more fun to try to see what other people in the train are reading than reading what you have brought yourself.

Especially when what you have brought to read is *Geography and Plays* by Gertrude Stein which you want to like very much but cannot latch one thing after another so quickly when what follows does not follow.

I walked from the room of white oceans to the room of black ink through the gates of yarn to the chambers of bent iron.

Is it so simple as having a code to break or can you lie down and close your eyes.

I lay down in the graveyard, hinged there. Closed my eyes and then.

On the train I looked down into a man's shopping bag. On the top was a pad of paper on which were written at least eleven different statements.

One of them said, "When you can't take life anymore, think about the alternatives and then deal with them instead of running away."

When I read "take life" I thought of the man as someone who had killed other people and was trying to rehabilitate himself.

The inside meets the outside in breath.

Where is God. Closer to you than your inhale and your exhale said the Imam.

But I wrote myself down in notes here, the night's cold I reached for me, reached for me and spoke.

Got one million things and another, a tattoo that was delicately airbrushed away.

You write it in your skin, a zero on one shoulder, an infinity symbol on the other shoulder — are those the ways you could go back there if you could.

To that knot of water, the place the river curls around yourself, where you learned to breathe.

Where you wrote out sentences and made them clean.

A boat on shore. The river cloud. All the secrets you heard and the things you wished.

Sounds from the apartment next to you used to keep you up all night.

So skinny you almost weren't there. But you wanted it.

Wanted to disappear.

A wind or sun of winter, the only son. Opens his mouth and no sound comes out.

Don't tell about the five months you never called home.

It was right after Dad showed you and Farrah pictures of a brother and sister who lived somewhere — Chicago perhaps. He was excited, hopeful some root would take hold, you would seed.

You both walked away from him, unable to speak.

You left home and didn't call.

Mom called you in May and you both pretended nothing had happened. That there hadn't just been five months of silence.

Yet still you manage to write about distance as if you didn't spin it into wheels.

You wanted it.

I sat across from my parents at a restaurant just a month ago, desperate to speak. I went there with them to speak.

And found myself suddenly deciding: too many years have passed. It has all been too long.

In Rhinebeck I lived where the river turns around and heads back to its source. Where the river returns to the ocean.

Breathing in that town, stretching yourself out and pulling yourself in at once.

How could you not understand.

On the stove brown rice, *daal,* and kale with garlic. Coming back with my roommates from yoga class.

But my body doesn't feel clean or correct, instead buckled up, strained.

To walk for an hour in the morning clears my head.

Walking through the neighborhood.

Everywhere I have lived since Rhinebeck I tried to recreate that place.

A small little town where everything was. Going from place to place and knowing everyone.

Having eaten well and breathed better the strength of those little years.

Forgetting to tell of the dark night I was locked out, or the dizziness I could feel over and over again unsure of where I was.

Still in the graveyard I lay down.

The day of the "leaving-home" I sat down.

In a room full of empty chairs I selected the one next to the only other person in the room. A gardener. Name of Marco.

Did I learn myself then.

Did I learn the way breath moves into and out of a person, and that a body is only a place the soul coalesces.

Or is it the other way around, the body like an antenna. The body the real thing pulling the soul-essence of the universe into its house.

I always think about going back and going in.

All the same.

Or is it.

Later that afternoon, convincing Marco to come back to town with me, take a walk through the streets.

At some point, for a moment, I took his hand.

Those moments against the years as you unsummon, unfold, uncry.

I have to tell you the most amazing thing.

You really don't know yourself so well.

CAIRO

In Egypt I asked why words exist we cannot pronounce. Asked as
Egyptian people mispronounced words like: Egypt. Pyramid. Sphinx.

Where are you from, the young tourist-police official asks me at the gate
of the Egyptian Museum.

The guard looks so young — he's a boy of seventeen or eighteen, a black
machine gun slung over his shoulder.

I am Indian, I say, nervous by how close his face is to mine.

If you are Indian, he says slowly, leaning closer, putting his hand on my
bare upper arm, where is your elephant.

I do not know any of the rules of communication here. Is he flirting
with me. Am I danger. Or is he trying to be funny or friendly.

In the one place everyone looks like me — has my name — I am the
most foreign.

An eternal sense: ever since there's been history — a telling of what
happened, there have been people who have lived at this river, at this
place.

The city as we drove from the airport seemed to become
monstrous — from the plane it stretched horizon to horizon.

The cities of the past — all built geographically on top of each other, but
also historically, culturally, linguistically.

There is no such thing as a "present" moment, nor of "this city"

The people I see walking down the street exactly resemble the figures in the papyrus paintings, in the carvings.

As it comes close to opening time, the workers begin to disappear to their jobs — the security guards, with black-irised eyes, and long lashes, dressed in bright white, hefting their black guns casually, unbelievably young, remain on every corner.

This book is sewn together. I am without language. The streets are so busy how will I get across the river?

The week before I left for Egypt I took the fast-boat from Boston to Provincetown. The boat was going so quickly it skipped on the surface of the water.

I've come to forget the years of joy.

You're a thread lost in a labyrinth.

You will drink from the river.

In the labyrinth the creature becomes not itself.

You've forgotten the thread, bull-man, wolf-man, fox-man . . .

There is a river in the labyrinth, Nile or Hudson or anything else you can name.

In Clarence once, at the height of winter, the snow two feet deep, seventeen wild turkeys picking their way through the yard, heading towards the house.

A labyrinth of time ties you back to the streets of Cairo, months after 52 men were arrested on a floating nightclub, taken to jail for crimes against society. Their trial will stretch out.

For years.

Such is the wandering and searching for the shining thread.

You will not forget the way out.

You will forget the way out.

In Paris I first saw the work of Nicolas DeStaël. In Egypt I wished I thought of him.

"One simply cannot think of any object whatsoever, because there are simultaneously so many objects that the ability to take them in falters and fades," wrote DeStaël.

I never knew if a bird or history or pharaonic. Never knew pyramid or the glass lid of the bottle.

Held at the center of the hotel like a prisoner.

What willful or wander waited.

Evening. At Stonecrop Gardens. Marco and I had dinner at Café Maya. Earlier we walked through the gardens, down the Himalayan Slope, to the bamboo grove.

How can I pick poems other than by heart? What do I really want to share with people? Not of my methods but of myself?

It's strange to look at what I've chosen for the manuscript I'm calling "the Far Mosque," sliced up, divorced from all the hundreds of other pages that went along with it. It feels like an excerpt of a book that never existed.

As if I ever existed.

Egypt was a concept or a country. I never saw it, never took the bus down the river to Alexandria, never wondered.

After *The Far Mosque* was published I learned about the controversy: whether the actual Al-Aqsa in Jerusalem is the "far mosque" of the legend, being described only by its adjective.

It didn't matter according to Rumi, who said something like, "the farthest mosque is the one within."

Days I wandered on my own; Salah, the driver assigned by the company to my father took me where I wanted to go.

Mohammed, the Egyptian man with an Austrian mother sat with me in the steam room of the hotel.

Salah took me to Cairo Tower, to the museums, offered to take me to the Sunni mosques and for some reason I did not want to go.

In the ether time of my childhood when I learned to speak I learned to recite syllables whose meaning I did not know.

Any teacher of a sacred text will tell you when he's teaching you that pronunciation is of utmost importance and that the power of the word is inherent in the unknown language itself.

Why, for example, *namaaz* must be recited in Arabic or the vedantic chants spoken in Sanskrit. Or Talmud remain in Hebrew.

It is not a mere theoretical distrust of translation but another form of distance from G-D, who if truly omnipotent or omnipresent must exist without language which even in its mortal form functions as a form of distance — necessary perhaps — from meaning.

I am on a rescue mission.

Dad and I went to the Coptic Quarter, down the narrow stone streets we make our way into a church-yard with no church.

In the subterranean church I wondered and fumbled for my father's hand.

Where are we and who are we.

Nine days later down the coast of dark countries, threaded by the wheeling stars, angel undone, light comes up.

The light opened onto shores and not onto open sea.

What shores are these.

The stars will not say.

Misread the characters of my name; for "patience" read "generous" or "divided."

The terrain shifts to thunderous mountains.

This is where you forgot yourself.

Where you slept for twenty years.

Storm clouds gather and settle along peaks.

The air is liquid with jags of lightning.

You are a sleeping rosetta slid between the liquid lightning and stone peak.

Wake up wake up cross the bridge into another country.

We took the car down to Saqqara one day where there is a step pyramid, older than the three at Giza.

The entrance through the Temple of the Sun, which having no roof now is truer to its name as a ruin than ever as a temple.

As I stood in the sand-yard in front of the pyramid soaring above into the pale blue desert sky I looked west into the dunes.

The desert in that direction stretches thousands of miles, all the way to the Atlantic.

A pit is so deep I cannot see the bottom in the ruined city of the wind.

Monument wake to me what is ancient and built.

Were we there.

I uncover a layer of hieroglyphics at the bottom of the wall, clearing sand away.

Every tomb has a watchman.

That magnificent pale, dusty blue sky. The color otherwise only ochre.

Imagining the previous life in the city behind the pyramid, not a necropolis but the ruined walls and foundations of an ancient city, a city before this place was desert.

Dreaming of the sweet watermelon from breakfast.

Ramses broken, lying down in the eroded empire, ringed by European and Japanese tourists on the second floor, looking over the railing.

It keeps these monuments in the immediate present — sacrilege also the way we walked amongst them, graffiti scarred, people touching everything . . .

Hard to discern what was original and what was reinforced construction.

In this way the ancient is lashed to the present but simultaneously kept ancient for public consumption.

I feel I am wandering a labyrinth but without a center, a bull, a thread.

The terrific beauty of the young man in the church, sitting in the pew next to me, his hand resting lightly on his leg, the violence with which the priest took the candles of the schoolboys and blew them out.

Earlier as we were driving through the valley to the beautiful beginning of Memphis I thought: here is the ancient kingdom of Kemet — just beyond Saqqara, the desert's edge — the magnificent first view of the kingdom from the desert.

On the way back from Cairo several workers were taking turns swinging from a tree into the river. I watched one, laughing, shaking his dark curls, grasp the rope and swing wild over the water. His white shirt wet against his chest.

I have to be able to say it.

In June of 2001 I went to Cairo, Egypt. All this was written during a decade of nearly continuous air raids and bombing of Iraq, the birthplace of civilization and of written language.

Osiris was torn into pieces by his brother; Isis traveled the world in search of the fragments to reassemble him.

And they said: oh Lord make spaces to be longer between our journeys ... so We made them stories and scattered them with terrible scattering ... most surely there are Signs in this for every patient grateful one (the Morning 19, Quran)

Layla al-Attar, the Iraqi painter, was killed when her house was struck by one of 23 Tomahawk missiles President Clinton launched at Baghdad in June of 1993 in retaliation for an alleged previously planned attempt on President Bush's life. Details of that plot have never been uncovered or proven. Al-Attar's home was reduced to rubble, her husband killed, her daughter blinded, and much of her work destroyed.

The libraries of Baghdad disappear into flame and smoke. The clay tablets smashed. Qurans burning.

I am writing you this from the past —

From "Thorow" by Susan Howe: *And what is left when spirits have fled from holy places?*

Valley riven the early year. Shift the plates and carve.

Cairo: an ancient statue of the Pharaoh next to statues of revolutionary heroes of the twentieth century.

An old Coptic church near an Arab mosque built over Greek ruins.

A ruined Roman aqueduct threads its way from the Nile to the citadel of the Turks.

Howe: *I thought I stood on the shores of a history of the world where forms of wildness brought up by memory become desire and multiply.*

Yet the hieroglyph does not unfigure. At a time when brutal strategy is employed in a war against the Arab people in the name of Western financial interests I went into the city looking for untranslatable icons. The Egyptian people, having Arab tongues, cannot correctly pronounce particular words tied into their mouths: *Pyramid. Sphinx. Egypt.*

My language buckled into my mouth, unbuckled itself.

Howe: *in the machinery of injustice my whole being is Vision.*

Faltering perhaps, fading for sure, though I mispronounce myself, I will speak.

NEW YORK CITY

At the end of my years living in the City I didn't know how to make a sentence anymore. I had a deck of index cards I carried around in my back pocket. It was May.

When a thought occurred to me I would write a line or two on a card and then shift it to the back of the deck.

On my way to work I would walk between an academic building and the big library.

There was a small steeple mounted on a pedestal, part of the original library.

Cities are like my deck of cards, one line after another, one thing and then another disappearing.

Piece for a trophy, the summer the debate was about whether or not the university would demolish a brownstone Edgar Allen Poe had lived in for six months.

What made history into a building?

When only the outside of the structure was the same and the inside had long since been refurbished into offices with drop ceilings and fluorescent fixtures.

I lay down on the little futon to read *Finnegans Wake*. Night after night I read *Finnegans Wake* to sleep.

By day I did yoga and kung fu and studied dance.

I woke early in my apartment on John Street and drank dark coffee and ate toast and white fig jam for breakfast.

Caught the 6 train up to the Village. I was in exile, living out of a suitcase in a completely empty apartment in the deserted money district.

On little cards I wrote a line and then another line in order to suspend the idea and pull it apart.

But at the time my interest was in obliteration. What I want to do now is find myself somewhere or to disassemble into air.

At the end, like every place I have lived, I left quickly. I packed my things up and rented a truck and called Sean and Tim to come down from Boston and help me. And drove my things up to Rhinebeck. August 2001.

Mornings I rose with the feeling of hunger in my stomach.

As long as I could I held on to that feeling.

Dad told me about one hundred and four books supposedly revealed by God.

Books revealed not written means meaning there only needs uncovering.

Four are named in the Quran so he does not discount the possibility of others, in other nations, other tribes, at other points in history.

Logically assuming that everyone has to have a fair shake at liberation.

Close to what Krishnamacharya said when he said you did not have to have a vegetarian diet to be a yogi or even be a Hindu of any kind.

Or as the monks chanted at the *tokudo*: "vast is the robe of liberation . . . "

I carried the notecards because it seems the clouds existed in snatches in the sky.

That buildings grew from concrete the way trees grew from the grass.

On the sidewalk around Washington Square the concrete buckles up in ridges from the roots of the trees.

Reminding everyone that underneath the city there is landscape.

It didn't matter to preservationists that the Poe House was already gone inside.

Peculiar I need reminding about that at this moment, a December morning, in my apartment on Marble Hill.

But just one block north of me, beneath what's now 228th Street, a creek used to run.

Long since diverted when the canal was blasted through to the south of 225th Street.

Now waterfront.

But before the skyline was revised, before all the other part began, before the phone scorpioned in my hand.

I lived in the lower end of the island. Near Washington Square Park, though briefly, after I came back from Paris, with only my backpack and a hunger, I had to stay down on John Street.

Every day I went to the university housing office and asked to be moved back up to the Village. Russell advised me to go in and lose my temper, become angry and irrational.

Which I couldn't manage.

The apartment complex I lived in was the same complex Anaïs Nin lived in and Hans Hofmann.

Hofmann became my hero because his paintings were to me like New York: all foreground and background at once. Each changing positions as it liked.

Anaïs became my hero because her novels and diary were the same way.

Because you could not tell what was fiction and what was autobiography, what was poetry and what was prose.

To be in love like that.

Walking down the street and seeing a young man with dreadlocks and blue long johns on underneath his cargo shorts.

Sometimes a poem is enough to seduce you or blue long johns worn underneath shorts.

In a labyrinth you are supposed to keep one hand on the wall to your right so you will never get lost.

But lost when I came back before the buildings fell and the war started. Not for all the reasons I couldn't make sentences.

But rather that I had been alone for so long, had not touched another for so long, lived there in what I thought of as the center of the world but not in the storm.

In the storm's eye.

Street cleaner runs by and I wildly wonder if the car is parked on the right side of the street.

Every time I ran down to the street I forgot my key and locked myself out of the apartment.

That's the point: what I gave up, what I was capable of abandoning.

What I am unwilling to speak of except in confusion and flashback.

Parts of it should not have worried me. I needn't have worried about being alone.

I came back from France unclear about all kinds of things.

Language.

What I wanted to forget.

The way to say things.

Who I thought I was. And had been.

On John Street I could go to the expensive grocery store to get French jam and not be homesick. Also there was a bookstore just on the next block.

It didn't help me much to write because I was stubborn and wanted to believe that the ineffable could only reveal itself ineffably.

So on my return from Paris I got wilder because I was returned to English. I wrote poems illegibly with text across text, or in grids with lines running horizontally or vertically.

One poem had arrows pointing different ways and had two different endings.

In one ending Psyche turns to look. In the other ending my name is next to a blank space: "Kazim and ———."

Though I refused to meet anyone or to touch anyone, there would be a time I would lie down in the graveyard and Marco would lean down to me.

That second year in New York I wrote a letter to a teacher of mine.

Privately when I returned from class or from a reading I would write him page after page.

Alone in New York, untouched for a year or more than that, frightened and broken-hearted and wanting to write, "*You think my gait Spasmodic — I am in Danger — Sir.*"

There was another bombing mission in Baghdad that year. I remember it in the spring and feel enraged. I was reading Darwish's account of the destruction of Beirut in 1982 called *Memory for Forgetfulness.*

We have forgotten over and over again. It was never our city first to be destroyed.

And now as I write this Beirut has been destroyed again. Baghdad too. Two buildings in Manhattan.

The first steel beams of Freedom Tower are being planted into the graves of thousands a couple of blocks from where I hid once for those weeks.

What's uncovered in the ground, landscape or landbridge.

If there is a book that will teach us will we be able to read it or do we have to write it first.

To write not in a book but in loose pages or cards. Not to disassemble but to assemble oneself into oneself.

I live on a part of the island that is not on the island anymore.

A canal blasted through and the rubble taken to seal up the creek that ran to the north.

We were part of the island and then we were our own island and then eventually we joined the continent.

A city could be like that or a painting or a person too.

Dickinson sealing her name up in a smaller envelope, refusing to publish.

There was a letter I wrote, kept in a folder of lost poetry, a letter I never sent.

PARIS

In New York I wrote on little cards to explain what had happened in Paris.

Walking along the Seine I remembered Melissa who said, think of me when you're there.

As if by imagining her I could bring her to me, the mirrored bands of water, the thickly gessoed sky.

The first bed I bought for myself was in college after I moved out of the dorms.

When I slept in that bed which had long belonged to someone else I felt I had dreams that were not my own dreams.

I could not describe them except to say I held a knife in my hand which was a real knife, one my mother had given me for my kitchen when I moved out of the house.

And that there were words written in fire on the wall of the bedroom.

But I didn't want words graven in fire.

A river I have lived along. Long since I lived the river.

The first night I left the apartment on rue Tiphaine and walked through Champ de Mars towards the river.

The streets wet with asters and deletions.

On the bridge across the river to the Trocadero gardens a street artist was drawing a young French man in charcoal.

A crowd had gathered around to watch the beautiful lines of his face appear shadow by shadow on the blank paper.

His irises were nearly black like an animal's.

I imagined myself in that crowd of people. What I wondered about the young man — that his face was so beautiful, eyes so open and clear — I wondered if my father had ever wondered about me, about my face.

He wrote in Arabic script on one of my sister's paintings, "You face is like a flower."

It's my face I dreamed he said that about.

I wanted to stay and be lost. Who doesn't want to drown in the beauty of another.

Underneath the bridge the river in the corner of the city I had never been.

Within a couple of days of arriving I had the practicalities taken care of: francs in my pocket, a subway card, a library card, enough basic French picked up from the airport to center of the city I could find my way around.

I knew where Gertrude Stein had lived, where Sartre and De Beauvoir were buried, Duras.

At the cemetery I saw an abandoned mausoleum, its doors lying open, the shelf inside empty.

A stained glass window above broken, the crack letting through a slice of the sky's actual blue.

Blue why I couldn't see the prison torn down or why I could see the cathedral.

Certain when I went to Chartres that all the stories about the Veil of the Virgin were true.

Bones scattered and saved in gold reliquaries and hidden in crypts.

I realized I had better apply some thought to the question of God and what He wants from us.

Being for the moment more interesting to think about that than what we want from Him.

Because if there was actually a Veil of the Virgin and I believe that much, believe it from seeing a cloth purported to be the Veil in question.

Then.

When we walked under the bridge I heard rain and other reasons.

Here disappearance you followed the sound of drums across the river to the Trocadero.

All kinds of people had gathered on the plaza overlooking the river and the tower. There were a couple of vendors who had spread out blankets on which to sell small crafts.

The drummers.

No one was dancing and though you wanted to dance you did not yet speak that language.

Beneath Paris a necropolis. Like a rumor of hallways and hallways of bones, arm bones and skulls and leg bones, whole chambers of pelvic bones.

A rumor also that the digging under the city nearly caused a collapse of the streets and so the bone-houses were abandoned.

They are not really there, I was convinced. You couldn't really find them. It couldn't possibly be true.

I found myself at a party full of my cousins' friends, barely any of them spoke English. I fussed my best but could hardly communicate anything, yet I found myself trying to say the most complicated things.

Is that why my sentences broke into little phrases. Because I could only say in English what I had syntax for in French.

You don't really know yourself so well, you know.

I dragged my cousin to any museum you could think of: Musée d'Orsay, Louvre, Centre Pompidou, Musée Picasso. And he took me to a couple I wouldn't have known to find: Musée Marmottan, Musée Rodin, Musée Zadkine, the Palais de Tokyo.

Only through art, not my own body, could I keep myself breathing.

At the Palais de Tokyo I saw a scraped wall and dirt underneath it from workers' boots.

Not so different from the impromptu extension of power tools and extension cords the workers at the Dia: Beacon Museum left there as a joke before the opening. Which remained for weeks during the opening exhibition before a curator noticed and had them removed.

On the broken sidewalk leading up the hills.

L'Idiot being the one book Catherine reads and re-reads every year. She went to Brentano's to fetch me an English language copy.

Who is there still if Melissa could ask me to think of her as I walked along the river.

Who is thinking of me still.

I am not a furious thinker. I stood at the bar sipping my drink looking here and there.

Trying to figure out if it was true you can sleep in the bookshop in exchange for working there. Strange I should meet in the shop someone I know from New York.

We make plans to meet that evening around the corner for coffee. While sipping she tells me about the necropolis below the city.

I didn't know anything but what do you know.

That it is such a short distance from Rouen where Jeanne was burned to Giverny where Claude Monet surrendered his sight.

Though blind and unable to discern color he continued to paint. I've seen the proof of it — nearly twenty canvases, monstrous, hanging in permanent exhibition at Musée Marmottan.

In the stairwell his palette is framed and hanging.

Brilliant light like Hofmann's.

You are light walking away from the river as if it were the Hudson.

Or wishing the words could flatten themselves into your mouth and you could speak strangely.

Speak God that stranger who undid you.

Build down the smoke in your understanding to the short bursts of excitement that come through the window while you try to write in English what's happened.

What's happened is France has won the European Cup and it's as if half the city has rioted.

Whose riot to understand and who riots now when what you wish is everyone to get more quiet, forget at least their fury.

Should fury spell France for you.

Still the rage inside you has found no way to leave.

But I left to go see what I would find if I found myself alone.

A second city that could spire itself.

Sense made the place and it's so obvious.

The francs in my pocket are littered not with politicians and slave-owners, but with Auguste Eiffel, Paul Cézanne, Claude Monet, Marie Curie.

Because it is a full color bill there is a little Cézanne painting on the reverse side.

I want to go where I could look at things that weren't supposed to look like anything.

I'm uncomfortable going home but I know I can't stay.

You wanted to dance but you did not dance.

I had a thousand dollars in my bank account. I emptied it and changed it all to francs when I got here.

When the money runs out I have to go home.

In pieces I wrote all this down, in pieces of water I rained myself down.

Helpless in a country whose language I could not speak I decided no matter what happened I would never go home.

CORSICA

At the ticket office of the ferry in Marseille, an elderly woman asks
me in French, "Are you German?" which is her way of asking, "Are you
a foreigner?"

In this case fiction is more interesting than truth which is that I could
not get tickets on a passenger liner and booked passage on a cargo ship.

There is a chapter called "Marseille" that I do not yet write. It tells
of how I could not find the hostel on the map and wandered a
neighborhood for an hour. When I find it I meet Tobi who takes off
his necklace — a blue stone on a leather string — and ties it around
my neck.

"This stone is meant to bring friends towards you."

In Marseille I did not wander but lived.

This is the story of my summer yes wandering for an hour.

What have you ever done but wondered when you could go home.

When you can't go home because there is something you have not said.

When you say it you will not have a home any more.

And who will say it if you are not going to say it.

So there is no having a home for you except as a place you will not be
able to go.

The last day I was on the island I had gone to a little hotel on one of the
backroads leading up the harbor behind the public square in Bastia.

Exhausted from weeks of dragging my backpack everywhere and down to my last sixty francs I checked in, promised by the concierge I could charge the room on my credit card.

If it is true we are alone in the universe then there must be a moment at which the space-time relationship is not constant, a moment that could hold the reliquary of *I-haven't-said-that-yet*.

A city is the understanding that you have a notion to subdivide. That carving could act as a generative demand: release everything in you as a river.

That will flood to the source, rise in the air, transform and return.

In Arles I walked twenty miles to the sea.

A road twisting through the swamps of the Camargue, occasionally seeing a white flamingo flying low across the road.

Ask me once more to explain the starving act as generative diamond released arriver, recessive genes emerging suddenly, all the dark-haired children turning gray prematurely, turning out queer.

That last day, facing an inevitable return to Paris and then New York all I had money for was a ticket on the cape-bound bus which went as far north as Erbalunga.

Light travel seaward to the antiquated relationship between the reason I arrived here and the reason I fled into logic too hot to mask.

It's not too far on the bus to carry on to the other passengers about the solar eclipse, the solar boat, the sayer of riddles, the stripped monument, and still leave a little space for Mister Why-do-you-say-this-stuff to respond.

Hold water in your mouth instead of responding to Mister No-way-of-knowing-where-you're-going-next.

A man on the rock beach, a couple of years younger than me, thick brown hair nearly in dreadlocks, eyes like geodes, asking me in French if I had any marijuana.

Later after swimming I saw him and his friend smoking and realized he was asking me if I wanted to share their marijuana.

Some number of different useless geodes are revealed to refract — we, sun-borne or sunborn, remarkable, writers of strange symbols onto the walls of various temples, ask to hollow the terms of our agreement made under conditions of incredible duress, fractious, billowing, cut into the fact that light still leaps backwards.

It will become possible at some future point of history to say with fabulous imprecision that the universe's expansion is not — as was previously believed — constant.

But first I went to Corti.

Climbing the steep mountainside in a creaking antique rail car: his body, the memory of him, smooth nearly hairless skin, hard and sinewy with muscle, lying against me or inside me, making a space in my skin like the depression in earth after a boat has been pulled back into the water.

My fault that the earth opened, my fault I couldn't say anything.

Even if not in my brain, in my tongue, in my little cells I think I still tasted metal, thought I was talking against God.

God like a thread that sewed me into the world, or that sewed the sky onto my skin or into me.

Why plunge back into the never-lived.

If every universe is the universe, if I am there, leaving the train station in Corti, hefting my bag back on my back and walking up the road into town to the hotel to get a room.

Wanting to do nothing, see no one. The sky was purple in Calvi, but you can barely see it here. We are so high in the mountains that the fog in the street is not the fog but actual clouds.

In the stone envelope I thought myself to death.

I didn't leave the ghost there but claimed him, named him.

I wish I could say I named him but he was like smoke suffocating me, suffocating me and I couldn't say him.

The naked whisper, naked on the roof, sweating out what was going to intoxicate me, whatever I wasn't going to be able to spit out.

That's the stone roof that won't split, the clouds lying down in the streets, a little cup of coffee and a day late on arrival.

Still thinking about it when the national cycling team came through on the second stop on their marathon bike race across the mountains from Porto Vecchio to I suppose Aiaccu.

Seeing their bodies, ubiquitous, I only remembered his body.

Every town on the island has not two but three names: in French, in Italian, and in Corsican.

A young man, Belgian, twenty-seven, an engineer on vacation filled up the outline of your memory. He was lean like a bird and sullen. He sat at a table in the courtyard gingerly removing his hiking boots. Where his Achilles tendons were, bright red anklets of blood, his skin gashed open by the journey.

Achilles slew the youngest prince of Troy, dark Troilus by running him down on the fields and crushing him to death.

This after the rape of Penthesilea's corpse.

Caught by you phoenix, caught by you and flayed.

Reading Anne Carson's *Autobiography of Red*, I could barely breathe.
I am Geryon the red monster I thought to myself. I have three names,
none of them my own, none of them pronounceable.

One more way to trick myself because in this case I did the betraying
and I did the leaving.

I outran you on the plains of Troy and have ever since been miscasting
myself as Quinn the crushed sculptor, every sullen and confused boy I
see who can't make himself speak.

Lonely in the coffee shop with funny shoes and a bad haircut, avoiding
everyone's eyes.

And remembering my hands, cold cables around a shopping cart, winter
in Albany so cold there isn't any snow, shopping for myself, buying in
my hunger.

Shrimp cocktail in glass cups, eggs, cheese, meat, anything to fill myself.

Why go backwards in time, why paint yourself into a corner and
why that memory here in the mountains, or at the crossroads where
a promise was broken, suddenly that loneliness, suddenly.

But suddenly him, the student who came into the coffee shop wearing
a turquoise t-shirt not resembling me in any way other than his quiet
loneliness.

The next morning I left my small room overlooking the central
courtyard to walk up the road into the mountains.

Dissatisfied by the openness of the road I followed a side trail into the
brush and made my way to a tongue of rock jutting out over the valley
nearly equal in altitude with the fortress of Corti a half mile away to
my left.

I lay there to draw myself in the way I lay on the stone wall in Cassis breaking my word to the sky, breaking the news, breaking down, breaking the silence.

Painted a little painting of the valley on the rock as I heard the speech of it dissipate.

Am I a man made of fire or the one who yearns to be caught, crushed to death.

In the town, the steep cloud-wed streets. Stark blue sky and the shadows of the mountains I sat there wishing to evaporate into the air.

The path I had taken up to the tongue of rock had disappeared and so I had to scramble down the steep slope, pierced by branches, stumbling into the dirt.

On the road back into town, dirty, unkempt, a disaster, I saw the small altars created in the crevices with flowers, candles, letters.

Sites of death — either by crash on the ground or by falling from the rocky slope from which I had just climbed.

A boy held over the walls of the city by his ankles.

The picture of war, *Guernica,* covered in black drape before Powell's speech, to make things possible.

When I sat down next to the Belgian engineer, the matron put down a plastic basket of baguette cut into pieces with a ramekin of cold butter chunks. Complimentary breakfast, the hotel's placard promised.

We spoke very briefly and neutrally about his trip.

For me each word we spoke was breath pressed painfully against his body, pressed painfully against the outline of the depression the boat left in wet sand.

In Calvi I met Amalla and Oihana from the Basque country. Looked up at them at the dinner table because Oihana used a Spanish that sounded so lilting and accented.

A school-teacher and a flautist with the Basque Symphony, we went up and down the coast together in the little car that they had ferried over, to Piana, to Ile-de-Rousse, other places.

Oihana spoke only Spanish and Basque and a speck of English; Amalla spoke only Basque and Spanish and French. So we made a friendship in my poor Spanish and my slightly better French, two of them translating back and forth in Basque.

English became very small and fit into the crevices and corners, all the secret places.

Where I build my altars to unspoken deaths.

From crashes on the road or falls from the rocky slope I had just descended.

PARIS

Your little canvas, *a little autobiography littered on the surface.* The way you first started swearing: on your back on the stone fence in Cassis, overlooking the stretch of mountains into the water to the calanques that spell you.

Fingers spell down your back.

Or spill.

Taking the nightboat to Corsica, waking up in another country.

Drunk year, stone year, tell it all backwards so what's before comes after.

You'll manage it that way.

I came to believe when I went into the cathedral of Chartres, raven in the field, to see the Veil of the Virgin. Came to believe the point is not to see through the thing that separates us but that the thing itself that separates is part of the point.

Coming through the dark crowds I thought to myself it was a hoax, the foot of a saint or something like that.

I said if it is fake it will be rich, blue velvet, embroidered with stars, but if it is real —

Struck the sun sinking, the trees amber, ember of flowers, the membrane of skin, the stains of last year's yearning, an urge of opening, on the verge of saying —

What must such a cloth look like?

Blue long since faded, embroidered stars unraveled.

In the wind along the road to Chartres, but here too — where's here —
or on the walk through the Camargue from Arles to the sea.

White threads reaching backwards.

Catherine tells about her pilgrimage from Paris to Chartres following
the medieval route, some pilgrims walking, in the old custom, on their
knees.

There, on Tuesday, between a raven screaming from the fields and a
walk through the cold labyrinth, and a bowl of garlic soup, I wanted to
see not through but at the veil itself.

I threaded my way through cities, from bookshop to bookshop, church
to church, and museum to museum.

How could I have come there and not believed.

At the chapel of Jeanne in the nave, a stone eagle bends to pluck grapes,
saints lining the spires.

Unwell at the chapel of Jeanne, lighting candles, in the dark recess two
ghosts.

One says "are you brave enough."

I could not say, I could not say.

The river moves too quickly, separated stream from bank.

In the shadows, bank of material for prayers: 5 francs for a candle.

At the chapel of the thirteenth apostle the sun comes through the
broken rose of lead and sand.

Thirteenth station of the cross the hand is cut on the candle, a jeweled box holding the bones of a British princess, Saint Ursule, splintered.

Dirt in my hands, dirt in my mouth.

What is the sound of blood vessels ripping away from bone, the breaking of the casket, the walls of the cathedral held up by thin shafts, iron straps of a ship trembling.

What is that sound we should not remember.

Braque: *La vase donne une forme au vide et la musique au silence.*

Novemberlight bent sideways and down, this is July walking down Champ de Mars to the water. A portrait painter on the bridge.

There on a small island, near Bartholdi's small model of the Liberty, I began writing in my journal in French, for five pages I wrote but only in the vocabulary I understood.

When I next switched back to English I found myself confounded by the boundary of the French in my head — unable to write more complexly than what I could express in the foreign language.

The condition followed me south on the train into the mountains of Corsica and back to New York.

It wasn't until years after that, when everyone started speaking in tongues that I.

Came to the house at Giverny to speak in tongues. In the morning we saw the scorched cathedral of Rouen.

Ruined. A gate to the garden, on the surface of the pond a dark shine.

The windows of the cathedral had all shattered during the war and been replaced by clear panes, the nave flooded by light.

Underneath the shine in the garden of a painter, a better pilgrimage site than any other, I stay on the bridge, wait for the dark to rise up, cover the paths. Pull the house down.

In the Quartier Latin I wondered what quarter has torn. Feeling in pieces, I mean and not knowing why.

The streets break for the river, the river cut in the shape of an angel, an angel in the shape of the wings of a river, a halo of light.

Harsh rain strafing leaves from the trees, birds unwrapping from the rain-slick eaves.

But I am hardly at the beginning of what I want to tell you.

When I went into the meditation room with its white walls I lost track of sound in the hum.

I wrote letters on my arms and my ankles. How the body pulls long to look for a poem.

What poem in the afternoon, sitting at the bridge watching the river travel underneath.

Is that all there is to it, that and languages I don't understand.

Because one day, a winter afternoon, one day in seven years I am going to find myself mapping out the spaces into which I never spoke.

I will not only be saying it in the present but will be saying it backwards and forwards.

Ahead, the new world which I am going to find for myself, completely consequenceless and inconsequential.

But also the lonely one who wandered from rue Tiphaine to Champ de Mars, from Champ de Mars to Trocadero, down the rue des Eaux he dared himself.

Dared himself into the future to find himself, to say what he wanted, say who he loved.

He wouldn't speak and instead watched the wooden struts of the town break and disappear into the waters.

Imagine watching the town break and the small buildings fold down.

Paradise lies beneath the feet of your mother or does Paradise lie at all.

Paradise the perfect painting, the panel is unmarked, surrounded by dried leaves.

In smoke a figure moves, bright orange trees, mauve beaches, great blocks of color.

Behind the figure, sharp flashes of light, behind the light, rising emerald, a hillside studded with lemons.

This is you, a mirror caked in clear varnish.

You in the morning walking along the river.

For what have you come?

In the evening thinking about the day. W*hat did you see? What did you say?*

Clamping your hand over your mouth.

What did you think you would find here so far from your life?

This is you whispering into your own ear.

This is you refusing to hear.

If all the tongues fade to background noise you're left with what.

An idea you have to choose between one thing and another, between them hanging the veil, the syllable of your life you cannot pronounce.

Over the stone wall, sprays of fuchsia, the wind is cold and beautiful and you've walked too far away from the apartment.

What a battle in your mouth, washed in the evening.

Still the door is unlatched, the evening light left on.

Don't tell yet about when you spoke, about when you were told about your crime, punishable according to some, by death.

At the Rodin Museum you had no money and tried to trick your way inside to those rooms full of figures emerging alive from marble.

You never got as far as the front door.

But linger in the garden

Sand marks the footfall, the approach to the great iron door.

And you start whispering, though too late, too late, *your back is a nation I have not visited* . . .

The sculptor with his dusty hands, mallet and chisel, a prisoner in bronze and black iron, a door to hell.

The light shines through the twisting figures.

One of them asks are you brave enough. To walk through the door to fire.

And what of the part of the sculpture which has been cut away.

What still of the rock left unquarried in the earth.

NEW YORK CITY

Suddenly with the light crashing down into the street, the white light of late-spring mornings, piercing the fog and haze.

Speaking opens me. I went to New York City alone and running away.

Running away and keeping secrets like a kid smoking a cigarette in the garage.

I had locks of green hair, hand-me-down clothes, a beggar, owning only a couple of bowls and couple of bucks, I hustled and who knows how it all came out at the end.

But I remember the strength of hunger, of pulling taut a hurting stomach.

Feeling at the thin edge between what and what.

Also not having anything, having to go to bookstores to read, having to borrow food and money, or going out with friends and pretending I wasn't hungry.

Once at one of those big group dinners for a friend's birthday I grimaced as the food came out, and the drinks. At the end of the night I put five dollars on the table because it was all I had.

Someone confronted me about it and I had to explain that I didn't have any more money and that I was sorry.

Later on the street, I stood apart, humbled and ashamed and somehow not angry.

I've left other cities out of this: San Francisco, Barcelona, Santa Cruz, Cold Spring. Missing chapters. All the things I won't tell.

Underneath the city of Barcelona the ruins of the Roman city of Barcino are still being excavated and preserved.

Under any city other cities still exist. Under any body other bodies.

Cold Spring is the place a giant chain was rigged across the Hudson River so the British navy would not be able to advance past to the northern towns.

In Santa Cruz the mountains fall into the sea.

But I came to New York to write poetry though unable to speak.

Because of this, wrote about ink tablets, about tables, about the threads that went from my skin into the air around me.

Late night phone conversations with Jason, sore from a day of running, or yoga, or kung fu, or dance, I would lie on the hardwood floor of the bathroom vestibule and talk with him.

Unable to say: I've made a mistake. I choose myself.

Still he was gone, in California.

Years went by longer than years.

I tracked the story back into words that were not words, letters comprised of magnetism & fiber optic. How each day would be a harbor to hold his letters to me.

How first he was only a story of a friend: her student had moved into my old apartment. He was exactly like me under his skin.

To seduce him, she had given him a poem she claimed to have written for him: which she had written, in fact, for me, five years earlier.

I never expected to take such a long journey, though I always said, and always believed that there was something about the length of my life written into his skin.

Strange envy in me: being some years older than he, knowing the longevity in his family, and the cancer and early death in mine, I settled on an arbitrary number that he would outlive me by.

By twenty years or more I figured, strangely choosing the seventies as my last decade and thinking he would last almost to a hundred since he eats so much whole grain, and so many fruits.

I envied his small bones, like Calder, not a fleshy body, but spindles hanging in space.

Speaking the language of the grass, the strange weeds, the pollen in the air.

Now he is journeyed back into story, beside the ocean, surrounded by sun and the arms of a new lover. I am writing to him only poems of journeys, poems I could not possibly send.

A new lover saying to him things I could not possibly have said.

My first look at him I had been waiting for an hour in the gallery café, having fought my way through throngs in the streets of Washington, DC, to be on time to meet him.

I didn't even know what he looked like.

But I am getting ahead of myself or behind myself really.

Meeting in the flesh so many months after silent messages across phone lines.

We would walk through so many different cities, writing to each other for a month or more before finally meeting.

Since we lived far away from each other our life unfolded in little episodes.

He waited for me at the Greek diner in New York eating baklava and translating Chinese characters.

The streets of Madison, Atlanta, Chapel Hill.

One night he scattered rose petals across the sheet, made sushi one weekend. When I sprained my ankle he gave me a potion of comfrey root.

He is too far away now for me to jump on the midnight train. Even too far away for me to call late at night.

He painted a picture of two little boys on the wall of our apartment in Washington, DC. An Arab boy with dark eyes in a keffiyeh and a Quebecois boy with curly hair in a red shirt and black shorts.

He moved out before I did. And so I was left with the task of painting over the little mural. Applying coat after coat until every trace disappeared.

Because I couldn't say it, to myself, to him, to anybody, I couldn't tell why I had been with him, why I had left him.

After Washington, after I went home to Buffalo, lost twenty pounds, became obsessed with running miles and miles and miles.

Now, years later, I wonder why no one could see my deep sadness, my desire to disappear.

Either I lied so well or they never looked at me, never saw, never wanted to see.

What was written in my face, written in every place of my body as it moved.

The memory of his hands, his tongue, his smile, his voice. I gave it all up willingly. Out of fear.

I did not even dare ask the question of myself.

No I do dare.

What did you think was happening.

Did you think that sadness was the natural state of my heart.

So having cut my body off from another body, having closed its flower to what it loved, I spent two years in Buffalo running myself to pain and smoothness.

And came to New York to what. To I believe turn myself away from the home of my parents and towards where I would go next. Rhinebeck.

Where in another year I would meet Marco.

It's easy to see when you look backwards.

Here backwards I looked in the rain, backwards through the streets and the stretch of my body.

Go down and greet them the ghost-pages that gather thickly in the clouds to flurry.

It's how you cultivate New York in your mind.

From the foreground to the background we moved against it, trying to see the world in planes or parts, trying to hear a single voice in the city.

In New York I wandered the rim of Washington Square at night, sort of friendless so I had nowhere to go and no idea of a good time on a rainy evening except walking up to the Strand.

What always speaks New York to me: a sidewalk, buckling and breaking under the pressure of the tree's roots growing through concrete.

And also my loneliness, my prowling the East Village bars late at night but going home alone.

The rain and me hurrying home alone, knowing no one will be there waiting for me.

And how that loneliness and also my hunger cleansed me.

You have no idea.

Where the bookstore was a high-end grocery is now. I still sometimes go in there and stand in the frozen food section — where the poetry shelves used to be.

Looking both backwards at something that was but also what I was thinking when I was that man, hungry, alone, nearly heartbroken, but also looking forwards at something — perhaps at me at this very moment, a lonely person dreaming of his future self, looking back and dreaming of him.

We are three points on a line.

As I wrote in a journal years ago, I had "the memory of a book I myself write next trying to say something that is true — "

BUFFALO

You came to the desert, spirit-ridden, illiterate, intending to starve.

And I did, I think, intend it.

Came pushing food away and allowed myself to shrink and shrink, to become thin and long like a bone or like Brancusi's wing.

Came then to love the look of an empty wooden bowl, what I imagined as a visual metaphor for my own stomach and my own life.

Waking mornings early I would make a cup of coffee from the jar of instant sitting on the counter.

I worked in the office of a factory and drove there, drinking my coffee from a plastic glass.

Kept myself by various means including Dostoevsky.

Whose *Crime and Punishment* became the first book I had to stop reading halfway through because it was too good. *Wuthering Heights* being the second.

But I came with my mouth open and panting, unable to say about the end of my life with Jason.

Unable to say how I had cut his hands from my body.

We let each other go with unsound explanations, and I came back to Buffalo alone, my body starving itself, sometimes barely able to stand upright.

I lost myself in Dostoevsky and Brontë: the Colonel shooting himself, Ganya leaping into the fire after the rubles. Catherine raging herself to death. Characters driven by insane passion.

I knew what insane passions felt like: Jason's hands shivering down my spine, Jason in my mouth.

But not what it meant to be driven by them.

Rather I was driven, a snowdrift, by the disbelief and shock in my mother's voice and against it my own desires held no sway.

I throttled myself and became thinner. And then thinner.

But what good is it to speak if truth in space is only a sculpture designed to collapse.

Either way this won't take back the years of silence, won't erase the annotations in all the scriptures, won't convince Ismail to stand up for himself.

Say: I will not go with you into the thicket. I will not lie down for the knife.

To say this now, after the turn of the millennia, after the cities went up in smoke, after the earth warmed and the ice shelf began to dissolve into the sea, what is there to risk in the last days of the earth.

The human body is a bundle of sticks in a chemical process similar to combustion.

As the skies broke apart from their moorings and fell down I strained against the ropes that chafed me.

Said Ismail, "Do as you are commanded. You will find me among the steadfast."

But alas this was not before the breaking of it before my courage evaporated into the space made in the air by my mother's grief.

I gave what I owned away and moved back home into my parents' house. I closed my mouth there and stopped speaking. I closed my mouth and began to starve.

You would think I gave poetry up for numbers, traded my body's urge for ignorance and obedience.

Everything I could have written might have ended there, in 1997, at the edge of the suburbs, my body demanding the only privilege it could: the miles and miles and miles I ran daily, weekly, through country roads.

There are three inside and one of them is this little complainer, the sweet boy, the ugly one, the shameful one who never knew how to ask for what he wanted, the one who sank down.

In New York City whenever I found myself alone but in a public place, for example taking an elevator, my knees would buckle and I would sink down to the floor, no longer having the strength even to stand.

So earlier in Buffalo, when I thought I might die in the most passive way possible — ceasing to eat — my body denied me, remanding me to the road, the endless runs.

After which I would come home, dehydrated and famished, and in spite of myself, or to spite myself, would eat.

Even now, trying to write backwards in time I can hardly think to look at the page, instead allow my fingers to move over it, marking it while I look up, stare across the coffee shop, out the windows into the street, or at people moving around the place, preparing for their meetings.

I use the present to understand the past is not finished.

Making it the future tense at the same time since I am writing backwards place by place.

What do I find at the end — a family I don't have anymore?

Or to understand that I do not bring this on my family the way they see it, a curse, a shame, a deviance, a crime.

I stripped myself down, left behind my job, gave away my things and left Jason to move back. To thrash.

Sometimes in public without prompting I would drown in the unfriendly lake I'd made of my own body and breath.

In a cubicle, in an office park, with an artificial lake and landscaped trees, in between a trip to the fax machine and an MIS training on computer security, I wrote poems in the margins of my papers.

The poems I wrote in the emptiness and silence were lessons and stories: especially Miriam the Prophetess, who became the central figure, the forgotten sister, became a woman by way of the apparent death of her brother, freed again by the blood-flowing river.

No one noticed my obsessions: poetry, endless exercise, and my refusals: to meet any of the women my mother and father selected, to eat meat, well to eat very much at all.

Jason moved out of the Washington, DC, apartment first and so the task was left to me to paint over the murals we had made on the walls.

Though I refused after his departure to stay in that apartment anymore.

Electing instead to move from couch to couch, staying a few days with each friend, as long as they could handle me staying.

That's the condition in which I arrived in Buffalo with only two suitcases and several boxes of books and miscellaneous possessions.

After eight years of living on my own, having my own apartments, furniture, kitchenware, that is what I was left with.

Then as now I belong nowhere.

I found myself unable to drive, to write checks, perform other simple tasks.

Every evening after working eight hour shifts in the office I would come home, run for miles, then sit on the deck and eat two pieces of toast with honey and a cup of green tea.

I read poems in the sun: Mary Oliver, Lisel Mueller, Agha Shahid Ali.

In this way I learned how a poetic line can be a support for grief.

And worse than grief is a grief one is unable to share. Living in a house after the end of a relationship considered illegitimate by the people who lived there.

This illegible wondering in the night of painting over the mural or the sundering of myself from another, who was a body in the country, who wrote there.

Of graveyards or Wednesdays in the gray at some point made strong and stronger from the running it decided first, before my intellect, that it wanted to live.

The third who is with them is always passive and was then also, watching dispassionately, wondering if I would wake up or lie down.

In the end I woke up by lying down.

I was offered a place in the graduate program in New York City but also offered a teaching position at a community college thirty miles away.

My mother of course, wanting me close, wanted me to take the job.

Another day of wandering, this one seemed to lend itself to wandering, journeying as I was from one city to another, following my work.

Each journey has its excuses for interruption. I filled my tank. Later, I stopped for coffee. Now I am thinking about a visit to a friend who lives out of the way.

I am pretending to stop again for coffee, but I am not thirsty. I approach the ice cream counter but it is only a pretext for the instinct in me.

I end up at the cast-iron sign detailing the purchases of the Holland Banking Company of the unsettled farmlands of Central New York. I pray to the details of history to know the reason the wind and my heart each wander.

Unsettled by whom? asks the wind scornfully, as my heart remembers the reason I wander and unsettles itself.

That summer I went away to Provincetown for a week to take a poetry workshop and while there I took a yoga class, my first.

When I lay down at the end of it, wrung out and strung out I sagged.

Everything leaked from me out into the ground and then back in. Out and then back in.

Remember what Lucille Clifton wrote, "she walked away from that hole in the ground, and decided to live. and she lived."

What proof did the third who is with them need other than the body that refused to die and the intellect that found its grief leaking its way into poems.

I went to New York.

WASHINGTON, DC

Georgetown. The late afternoon sun is dark as honey sliding down
M street in beginning of summer.

There is an Arab restaurant inviting Muslims to break their fasts behind
the high and metal doors.

The fourth of July weekend I should have returned home to visit
Ammi-jaan, sick with cancer for three months, I took Vietnamese
take-out to the small canal now covered with green, sat there reading
a comic book, thick in my loneliness.

Remember, we used to sit on the second floor of the bookstore, in
the café, looking down over the street, each with a stack of books. I kept
thinking I might find myself there, maybe knowing deeply that I would
stay lost.

Still, the sounds of talk and cars, the thick French soup, the warm wood
of the pier, Jason's soothing voice, always putting me together.

Jason loves to put things together.

The night I moved down to Washington, DC, driven by my elder sister
and my brother-in-law my right upper wisdom tooth broke in my
mouth. The shards stayed there for two more years before I could afford
to have a dentist pull it out.

It would be two more years before I would have enough money to have
the other three extracted.

The late afternoon sun is dark as beginning to break.

Behind the high and metal doors my home.

The small canal now covered with green.

Remember, we used to sit there together, reading.

Ammi-jaan had already died by the time I went home a month later.

Paradise lies beneath the feet of your mother.

My father, as is usual, read the services. "If any of you have a grievance against Jaffery Sayeed, forgive her for it now," he said, "and if she has a grievance against any of you beg her forgiveness."

Because I had not come home in time, because I never wanted to come home, keeper of secrets I was, I burst into tears and couldn't stop.

She'd left and turned to tell me.

What.

Nothing.

Afterwards I lay down in the bed praying for something real and for the silence to unfold its hands and show me.

There wasn't any way.

My friend wrote to me from Albany about a new student in her Greek class who reminded her of me in his torment between god and the body.

Having not yet realized there was a mind-self and a body-self inside me along with the third who is with them.

She flirted with him by giving him a poem she originally had written to me.

Which of us would play Apollo and which of us would play Dionysus. No one who knew us could tell.

Now I know Jason was more Apollo and more Dionysus both
than I ever was. If any opposite pair I am Persephone and Hades
who took her.

The myths do not write me though because I am I. There wasn't one
before me.

When I said what I said in the cold afternoon, when I said finally what
I needed to say in that house, my father asked me, Are you a Muslim?

Dumbstruck, I had no answer.

I am I, a driftless star, disowned from his own constellation.

Who will be able to find the polar star now?

How I become a man is an unwritten book.

Because finally, at the end of it, I am not Isaac who cried out in anger
against his father, but the other son, the elder one, the darker one.

The obedient one. The one who said, "You asked me to lie down and
I lay down."

Who said, "Father, if this is God's will, let it be done. You will find me
among the steadfast."

That's how it happened to the son who went into the desert with his
mother and father.

To starve.

Who knows how things fit and what you are supposed to say.

I know how things fit. You are not supposed to paint on your wall, but
we did, Jason and I.

He was an echo at first, an earlier version of me. If he was an earlier version of me then he was the one I wished I had been not the one I had been.

The one I had been: ugly, ashamed, frustrated, hedonistic, undesired.

A wretch really who flew from one room to another without any need or understanding.

Staying up late into the night, smoking cigarettes and wondering.

My friend, the classics professor, obsessed with phoenixes and nursing her own desires, saw Jason on the street once near her apartment. She too saw him as a version of me and walked behind him, following him into her own apartment building, a building I myself had once lived in when I was in Albany.

I met a million and one furies. My first experience being pressed against the earth.

A hot river to drown me or the plates of the earth moving apart and then together to crush me between them.

Have you ever been so thrown down, so twisted to disappear with liquid into the air.

She watched Jason walk down the hall with his keys and then unlock the apartment that had been mine: 92 Willett Street, Apartment 1D.

After they had become friends, after she had given him the poem, after she confessed it, after he and I started writing to each other, I wondered to myself if the dreams he was having, the conflict between his own spirit and bodily desires were mine somehow, left in the apartment, physical things.

It being a story of politics, he painted two little boys on the apartment in DC — a boy in an arab gelbab and keffiya and another with curly hair, red shirt and black shorts.

When he left I had to paint over this little mural, the failed echo of what I had tried to do — love regardless of my culture, my religion, the social pressure I faced.

When will I break the fast and tell the story of our silence?

Let me not leave it at the failure. I am traveling back in time for a reason.

Let me leave it that first day before I knew him, before I loved him.

He and his friends were traveling down to Washington to see the AIDS quilt. We had arranged to meet.

I was at a breakfast meeting. Leaving the meeting early I made my way down to the National Gallery of Art café.

Had to fight my way through a huge rally and march of striking custodial workers.

I got to the gallery early in spite of my adventures and sat there watching people walking in, trying to piece together Jason's description of himself, wondering which of them was he. Each time a person roughly matching his description arrived, in the seven seconds between their appearance and realization each was not he, I pieced together a whole imaginary life.

ALBANY

In the night that doesn't pass I saw a man crumple beneath another man's fist.

My instinct in a moment of crisis was not fear but rage and I ran screaming towards them.

Having always been a coward, always shied away from the most important bravery I was alarmed to discover my inner nature was not that of scholar or dissident but warrior.

The man rose with my help, well-built, handsome, a trickle of blood coming from his nose.

He was as shocked as I was, saying "I didn't see him. He hit me."

I was the slight one, the dark one, skinny and unsure, trained to obey.

Yet that night I was the one rescuing.

Arriving in the city of stone with my book and little else.

On February 8, 1990, I called my friend Nadya, unable to sleep, awakened by loud roommates. She invited me to stay overnight at her place downtown so I went.

We talked for a little while and she said I should keep a journal which I said I couldn't do because I could never write in it, lacking any discipline.

Nadya said, why do you have to write in it every day? Just get a blank spiral notebook and write in it when you feel like it.

My aunt told me that she keeps journal too, only she destroys them. She's saved only two: one is the account of her pilgrimage to Mecca and the other the journal of her period of convalescence in the hospital after serious surgery.

The two fragmented periods of her life, the parts she left written. Are they the real ones or the unreal ones?

Mom packed a small box for me for my first kitchen when I moved out of the dorms at the beginning of my junior year of college.

In it was a pot, several wooden spoons, some knives. I still have the pot, still have one of the knives, a wooden spoon.

Also she bought me a set of plates, bowls, cups and saucers that I still have most of. One bowl and one plate are broken, two cups gone missing, but the saucers are all still there.

I lived in a neighborhood beneath the Cathedral of the Immaculate Conception. My favorite places were Nepenthe, a vegetarian café, and a performance space called Artists for a New Politics. Both were gone within five years.

That winter was so cold, far away from campus, accessible only by the Wellington bus, a long walk under the highway for me. I'd separated myself because I felt my life was sinful and wrong.

Is that how it happens: one day you turn around a corner and your body is suddenly different and you want something you never wanted before.

How it all gleams and reminds me.

Cocooned in Mansion Hill, forgetting myself, I tried to write my first novel.

Eventually novels would evaporate to politics, politics would splinter into poetry.

I could finally start to see books as condensations.

The campus of the University at Albany, some said, was designed to be the University of Arizona, hence all the wind tunnels.

Designed after the government plaza of Tehran, others said.

Either way a place not a place, a place which had become not what it was destined to, a strange channeler of extreme psychic energy and distress present on any college campus.

When I sought to read it was either the landscape, the ocean floor, or the flat black page of the sky.

You seek to define.

And then a Plank in Reason broke—

Fine after coming I spoke to my advisor to change my major from Political Science to English, I no longer wanted to go to law school but wished to become a writer, her first question was:

"Have you told your parents this?"

I said I had.

And she said, "But did you tell them you wanted to go to the desert, that you want to paint it purple?"

Judy was also the first to teach me about Emily Dickinson, that her books had been broken apart, that her poems even in their "authentic" versions had been relineated.

So everything I knew had actually come through decades of editing and authorizing.

So it was possible after all for a suppressed voice, a redirected voice, a suffocated or strangled one, to still speak.

Classical Islamic arts refract individuality through form.

Geometry. Architecture. Calligraphy. Recitation.

You do not form yet you will make a space.

A space is not a silence but a promise.

When is a room the four walls that enclose it.

Is it possible to speak.

In Cairo, years and years from Albany, looking up into the tiled dome of the Sayeda Zainab Masjid.

Surrounded by pilgrims and praying faithful, yet understanding from my own studies that Sayeda Zainab never came to Cairo.

Died in Damascus. Was buried there.

I began to paint in Albany because I ran out of words.

It wasn't technique but the desire to express that led me to form after form of art.

Each form depending on the individual body and the individual body's expression. Poetry. Painting. Dance.

I painted on my own skin.

And shied away from art forms in which the individual sublimates himself to form. Photography. Music. Acting.

The form which joins these two opposites which I always approach and retreat from. Sculpture.

Picture this writing if you like as a sculpture.

I fell down and down —

Because there was no Muslim community to speak of on campus, Mom put me in touch with some people in the community. During Muhurram she told me I should go to their houses for the observations.

I didn't want to go and so I decided not to call them but I still felt bound by my mother's stricture. I called the day of the event and since no one could drive me I took a bus out to the suburbs.

They lived past the end of the bus route and so I ended up walking for nearly an hour through the housing development which had no streetlights at all.

Since no one was expected to be walking on the streets after dark.

When I finally found the house, illuminated from within, I entered without knocking, put off my shoes, and walked down into the basement uninvited.

This is where people had gathered and my presence was accepted without question.

I was given a ride back home into the city and upon walking into my apartment was greeted with the noise and laughter of the large crowd who had gathered there.

Rather than retreat, after the somber recitations, the silences of the ritual gathering, I went into the living room and sat down at the coffee table with everyone else, not really contributing to the conversation that I can remember, but needing, at that time, to surround myself with noise.

It doesn't matter that there I first looked at myself, there I learned to disobey.

The crime was not in my discovery of my self or in following myself.

If there was a crime it was in believing something different than my parents believed.

It was in leaving the house, leaving the family, deciding that my rules were different, my life itself was going to be different.

That's why I couldn't just break up with Jason and stay in Washington, DC to live by myself.

I had to leave my job, my apartment, all of it, and move back into my parents' house.

Buckle myself back into place.

And why when I couldn't rebel in any meaningful way, couldn't stand up for myself yet, couldn't say what I needed to, I could move myself away from them, and as a way of resisting notions of being "settled," I could keep moving.

From city to city, from job to job, anything to deny myself the appearance of being "ready": for marriage, for children, for an established presence.

Who can tell now, after twenty years of doing it, whether I wanted it or not.

I take joy from it certainly. Going between Pennsylvania and New York City, spending time during the summers and winters in Maine.

Disappearing once in a while to New Hampshire, to California, to any number of places.

Fliply but nostalgically thinking of Rhinebeck as "home" though I only lived there for three years and that too five years ago.

Hit a World — at every Plunge —

Strange to open this hurt now but I turned it out into the world. Raised in the middle class I became acutely aware of injustice and developed an analysis not yet based on class but on race and cultural difference.

To speak against the enemy when the enemy was myself.

That's really what Satan meant when he spoke to Jesus in the desert: I will give you all this if you fall down and worship me.

How easy it would be to do it: to bow down and worship the Satan inside: my hatred of myself.

Being a stone fallen from the sky, how easy also to turn my self and disappear into the world.

"I will give you all this," said the devil and meant either the material rewards of the external world or all the validations and gifts of a promised hereafter.

Neither Isaac nor Ismail, I am the third son, the wolf-tongued son.

So sure of G-D he is willing to walk through the door to fire.

HOME

My father had a steel comb with which with he would comb our hair.

After a bath the cold metal soothing against my scalp, his hand cupping my chin.

My mother had a red pullover with a little yellow duck embroidered on it and a pendant made from a gold Victoria coronation coin.

Which later, when we first moved to Buffalo, would be stolen from the house.

The Sunn'i Muslims have a story in which the angels cast a dark mark out of Prophet Mohammad's heart, thus making him pure, though the Shi'a reject this story, believing in his absolute innocence from birth.

Telling the famous Story of the Blanket in which the Prophet covers himself with a Yemeni blanket for his afternoon rest. Joined under the blanket first by his son-in-law Ali, then each of his grandchildren Hassan and Hussain and finally by his daughter Bibi Fatima.

In Heaven Gabriel asks God about the five under the blanket and God says, those are the five people whom I loved the most out of all creation and I made everything in the heavens and the earth for their sake.

Gabriel, speaker on God's behalf, whisperer to Prophets, asks God, can I go down and be the sixth among them.

And God says, go down there and ask them. If they consent you may go under the blanket and be the sixth among them.

Creation for the sake of Gabriel is retroactively granted when the group under the blanket admits him to their company.

Is that me at the edge of the blanket asking to be allowed inside.

Asking that 800 *hadith* be canceled, all history re-ordered.

In Hyderabad I prayed every part of the day, climbed a thousand steps to the site of Maula Ali's pilgrimage.

I wanted to be those stairs, the hunger I felt, the river inside.

I learned to pronounce my daily prayers from transliterated English in a book called "Know Your Islam," dark blue with gold calligraphed writing that made the English appear as if it were Arabic complete with marks above and below the letters.

I didn't learn the Arabic script until years later and never learned the language itself.

God's true language: Hebrew. Latin. Arabic. Sanskrit.

As if utterance fit into the requirements of the human mouth.

I learned how to find the new moon by looking for the circular absence of stars.

When Abraham took Isaac up into the thicket his son did not know where he was being led.

When his father bound him and took up the knife he was shocked.

And said, "Father, where is the ram?"

Though from Abraham's perspective he was asked by God to sacrifice his son and he proved his love by taking up the knife.

Thinking to himself perhaps, Oh Ismail, Ismail, do I cut or do I burn.

I learned God's true language is only silence and breath.

Fourth son of a fourth son, my father was afflicted as a child and
as was the custom in those days a new name was selected for him to
protect his health.

Still the feeling of his rough hand, gently cupping my cheek, dipping the
steel comb in water to comb my hair flat.

My hair was kept so short, combed flat when wet. I never knew my hair
was wavy until I was nearly twenty-two and never went outside with wet
and uncombed hair until I was twenty-eight.

At which point I realized my hair was curly.

My father's hands have fortune-lines in them cut deeply and dramatic.

The day I left his house for the last time I asked him if I could hold his
hand before I left.

There are two different ways of going about this.

If you have known this for years why didn't you ask for help, he
asked me.

Each time I left home, including the last time, my mother would hold a
Quran up for me to walk under. Once under, one would turn and kiss
the book.

There is no place in the Quran which requires acts of homosexuality to
be punishable by lashings and death.

Hadith or scripture. Scripture or rupture.

Should I travel out from under the blanket.

Comfort from a verse which also recurs: "Surely there are signs in this for those of you who would reflect."

Or the one hundred and four books of God. Of which only four are known — *Qur'an, Injeel, Tavrat, Zubuur.*

There are a hundred others — *Bhagavad-Gita, Lotus Sutra, Song of Myself, the Gospel of Magdalene, Popul Vuh, the book of Black Buffalo Woman* — somewhere unrevealed as such.

Dear mother in the sky you could unbuckle the book and erase all the annotations.

What I always remember about my childhood is my mother whispering to me, telling me secrets, ideas, suggestions.

She named me when I moved in her while she was reading a calligraphy of the Imams' names. My name: translated my whole life for me as *Patience.*

In India we climbed the steps of the Maula Ali mountain to the top, thirsting for what.

My mother had stayed behind in the house, unable to go on pilgrimage. She had told me the reason why.

Being in a state considered unacceptable for prayers or pilgrimages.

I asked if she would want more children and she told me the name she would give a new son.

I always attribute the fact that they did not, though my eldest sister's first son was given the same name she whispered to me that afternoon, to my telling of her secret to my sisters when we were climbing the stairs.

It is the one betrayal of her — perhaps meaningless — that I have never forgiven myself.

There are secrets it is still hard to tell, betrayals hard to make.

You hope like anything that though others consider you unclean God will still welcome you.

My name is Kazim. Which means *patience.* I know how to wait.

BARCELONA (AN EPILOGUE)

So having actually been able to speak.

Arrived or am arriving in the Catalan sun.

Narrow streets of the old city.

My first day deaf so thinking everything was quiet or a world away.

Dad's voice in my dreams first talking about death and then shouting
my name.

A silence from my parents and though I am still talking to my sisters,
we are not talking about this.

I came around the world to sort it out or did I come to begin another
sentence.

"All this will I give you if you fall down and worship me," tempted Satan.

Being lost in the garden, the idea of breath even in stone.

The feeling of loss watching the *sardana* dancers in the cathedral square.

Do I belong to anything?

I am not an orphan and even if I am.

If Paris seemed like water dramatically soaking my loneliness and
filling every space and Cairo seemed mere backdrop to my own
drama, traveling with my father, desperate to be touched, here seems
commonplace but in the beautiful sense of that.

I stayed deaf through the evening and into the next day.

Our off-center orange-walled room.

When sleep's strident voice shouted my name into the angry silence.

I've built a career on silence it seems.

A light accretion of sentences and waking up.

That first night in the cathedral square, musicians playing including one playing an odd wind instrument, reedy and brassy but thinner in sound and shape than a saxophone.

Circles of people dancing a slow and deliberate and seemingly very simple folk dance.

How I came to hear again in a baptism of my own loneliness.

My mental awareness finally apologizing to the joyful, sudden body-child, my visceral self, the part that's shy and gleeful always being beaten down by me for not being leaner, more beautiful, for not living up to some idea I have about what I ought to be.

The oldest part — the part that is me and isn't — was pleased to hear the thoughts of the mind in its sickness and the body weakly agreed to get better.

There is a place where the flesh of the body — the mind being ensconced within its cells and chemical reactions — and the self of the "immortal spirit" do not meet each other; a gap in each person, a place we do not connect and that, this lack, the earthly place we cannot get to being a metaphor for that, is a place of God.

We head into the old city every night — so many people in the narrow and crooked streets without the nuisance or primacy of traffic.

At the north end of the city in the foothills the monastery of Montserrat.

Rounded because once it was at the edge of the ocean.

Marco roams every place writing down the names of plants. He buys me rosemary candies at the market to soothe my sore throat.

I can hear again and am beginning to be able to breathe.

Is it still possible the shock of loneliness, the sweetbitterness of it.

On the southern border of the city, Montjuic where the Jewish communities once lived.

In the Joan Brossa garden we sat on a slope and ate oranges.

One little boy had lost his mother and was calling, somewhere between desperation and hysterics: "Mama! Mama!"

A woman in her sixties caught his hand and walked him through the park, helping him look. He was so distressed he walked into a lamppost and we had to suppress our laughter.

And I stop quickly, with sticky fingers, feeling like a boy myself, realizing that little boy is me, searching for his mother, but my mother isn't looking for me yet, doesn't know where to look.

Time is passing. Are we losing each other? Is it already too late?

Even after I said it I went to my room and began packing my things to leave immediately and my mother came into the room to say, "You don't have to leave. This will always be your house."

I realized I have lived in six cities in five years.

Climbing the stone staircase thinking am I an orphan now?

Each morning we opened the shutters and pulled small chairs out on to the balcony to eat fresh bread and cheese, eat oranges.

The wind lightly in my curls.

At the edge of the ocean the oldest part of me thinking always that the evaporating horizon — the sky and sea meeting each other — was proof of God but when Sakina and I went into the water after Chand Mumani's passing the sky was so purple, the water the most emerald green.

So separate objects sometimes do not find each other.

I'm proof of no one and no one's proof.

Beneath this city, the Roman city, its buildings and streets, centuries and centuries and centuries old, is still intact.

Home I have not or naught. Six more days with Marco in Barcelona.

I cannot hear but here.

Orphaned by sound departing, but words departing in air, water into the air.

The distressed child abandoned in the park calling for his mother, "Mama! Mama!"

I am a word and its mother, a city that's the seed of winter.

The child finds himself lonely for sound but angling for the empty shore.

This is what it means to button yourself to the lost year, your lost ear that resounds, you did not look back.

Only three people know where you went and not one of them knows how to find you.

Oh but how to find you.

In the blue tiled hallways.

On the dragon roof breathing.

Will you find paradise that lies.

Mother who lies at the bottom of the sea in the night I will find you.

But who am I lonely traversing the avenue from the mountain to the sea nightless in the day and dayless in the night.

I have not found the way to stitch myself to the seam of the afternoon that seems to open where water meets water.

A gulf or galaxy floods between an orphan and his mother.

At the gates of the old city the door to the ocean I knelt down and whispered a devotion to the decades of roof, to the cathedral.

On the cathedral steps the beggar was me.

Who can say what the steeple reached for angling to blue.

For you who spoke words against me first a question are you a Muslim, are you not yoked to either this life or the next one

Is that my wish then to be soaked then to be threaded to know geography and place to be in a place, actually moving through space.

In this place the narrow streets and courtyards of light, motorcycles parked next to the ancient walls all of us here are really citizens of wind traveling without papers in summer's bleached capital, rumpled travelers bored by exile.

Orange trees lining the streets.

Following the sound of a guitar around a corner, crushed oranges in the gutter.

Will I find myself or fine myself stopped in the street for stumbling for not living in a place not being bound nor bound anywhere to a family, nation, or god.

You cannot hear bound nowhere bound by nothing you are a letter fluttering away down the street toward the sea.

What tongue is yours.

None.

Are you a Muslim or will you love.

I will not answer.

All this will I give you if you fall down and worship me.

I will not choose.

Fathered by sound I am.

Kind mother your kin.

Kazim Ali's books include the poetry volumes *The Far Mosque* and *The Fortieth Day*, and the novel *Quinn's Passage*. A second novel, *The Disappearance of Seth*, is forthcoming in 2009 from Etruscan Press. He is on the faculty of the Stonecoast MFA program at the University of Southern Maine and is assistant professor of creative writing at Oberlin College.